GUATEMALA

TRAVEL GUIDE

A Journey through Ancient Mayan Kingdoms & Colonial Charm

Henry Brew

Copyright

All rights reserved. No part of this publication may be reproduced, distributed, or transmitted in any form or by any means, including photocopying, recording, or other electronic or mechanical methods, without the prior written permission of the publisher, except in the case of brief quotations embodied in critical reviews and certain other noncommercial uses permitted by copyright law.

Copyright ©Henry Brew, 2024.

TABLE OF CONTENT

INTRODUCTION

As the morning sun cast its golden hues over the vibrant streets of Antigua, Guatemala, I knew I was about to embark on a journey unlike any other. My heart fluttered with anticipation, eager to embrace the country's rich tapestry of culture, nature, and history. Guatemala, a land shrouded in the mystique of ancient civilizations and enlivened by the warmth of its people, was not just a destination on a map; it was a story waiting to be lived, a narrative to be woven into the fabric of my own life.

The cobblestone streets of Antigua whispered tales of the past, each stone a silent witness to the ebb and flow of time. The city, a UNESCO World Heritage Site, was a kaleidoscope of color and life. I wandered through its vibrant markets, where the air was thick with the scent of spices and the chatter of local artisans. Their hands, deft and skilled, weaved textiles of such vivid colors and intricate patterns that they seemed to capture the very essence of Guatemala's soul.

Venturing beyond Antigua, the serene beauty of Lake Atitlán took my breath away. Surrounded by volcanoes, its waters mirrored the sky, blurring the lines between heaven and earth. In the nearby villages, I encountered the heartbeat of Guatemala's indigenous cultures. Here, time moved to the rhythm of tradition, and I was privileged to witness the enduring legacy of the Maya people, their customs and languages are as alive today as they were centuries ago.

The call of adventure led me to the Petén region, where the ancient ruins of Tikal stood as solemn guardians of history. As I climbed the towering temples, the jungle canopy below me was a sea of green, alive with the sounds of howler monkeys and exotic birds. The view from the top was a moment of transcendence, a communion with the ancients who once gazed upon the same lush expanse.

But Guatemala's allure wasn't confined to its landscapes and historic sites. It was in the simple, everyday moments – the shared smiles with locals, the taste of freshly made tortillas, the rhythm of marimba music floating through the air. Each day brought new flavors, from the rich, aromatic coffee cultivated in the highlands to the zesty piquancy of Pepián, a traditional stew that warmed my soul.

In the bustling markets, I haggled over vibrant textiles and handcrafted pottery, each piece a story in itself, a connection to the artisan who crafted it. In the evenings, the streets came alive with the sounds of laughter and music, the communal spirit of Guatemala embracing me like an old friend.

What struck me most profoundly was the resilience and warmth of the Guatemalan people. Despite a history marked by hardship, their spirit remained unbroken, their hospitality unwavering. Their stories told with a blend of melancholy and hope, were a testament to the human spirit's enduring strength.

As I explored further, I delved into the natural wonders of Guatemala. The emerald expanse of the rainforest in El Petén, the mysterious depths of the Cenotes of Candelaria, and the volcanic landscapes surrounding Antigua were reminders of the Earth's raw, untamed beauty. Each hike, each boat ride, was not just a journey through nature, but an exploration of my inner landscapes, a reconnection with a part of myself long forgotten.

As my journey neared its end, I found myself at the vibrant Sábado de Mercado in Chichicastenango, a bustling market that was a feast for the senses. The air was thick with the aroma of incense, the vibrant colors of textiles blending with the earthy tones of wood carvings. Here, amidst the chaos and beauty, I realized that

Guatemala had changed me. I had arrived as a traveler, but I was leaving as a part of a larger story, a narrative interwoven with the threads of history, culture, and human connection that make Guatemala so profoundly unique.

To those who yearn for adventure, for a journey that transcends the mere act of travel, Guatemala awaits. It is not just a place to visit, but a world to be experienced, a story to be lived. Through its streets, its mountains, its forests, and most importantly, through its people, Guatemala offers not just a journey, but a transformation. Come, be a part of this story, and let Guatemala's magic redefine the way you see the world.

HISTORY AND GEOGRAPHY

The first people to arrive in Guatemala are thought to have crossed the Bering Strait from Asia 14,000 years ago, and there is evidence of human settlements dating back to around 9000 B.C. Around 1000 B.C., people started to cultivate and build communities. Some of these people went on to become the Maya, who ruled Guatemala from 250 to 900 A.D.

More than 1,300 years ago, the Maya temple at Tikal was constructed as a mausoleum dedicated to Ah Cacaw, the Maya emperor. Once home to 100,000 people, Tikal was a large metropolis that started to fall around the year 850 A.D. and was abandoned about 50 years later. It took till 1695 to locate the ruins.

The greatest surviving tribe, the Quiché, was attacked and subjugated by the Spanish in the sixteenth century. After being defeated, the Quiché were sent to labor on large estates in the recently founded province of New Spain.

Geography

Volcanoes, mountains, and beaches bordering the Pacific and Caribbean seas may be found in Guatemala. This little nation is distinguished by contrasts, from the Cuchamatán Mountains in the western highlands to the Caribbean and Pacific Ocean beaches. Of the thirty volcanoes in Guatemala, three are still active.

The most active volcano is Pacaya Volcano, which is close to Guatemala City. More than 84,000 years ago, a volcano erupted, creating a caldera that eventually gave rise to Lake Atitlan. At an estimated depth of 900 feet (300 meters), the lake is the deepest in Central America and spans 48 square miles (125 square kilometers).

Guatemala is a mountainous nation that is just slightly bigger than the state of Tennessee in the United States. A third of the people live in chilly highland settlements. The lowlands around the shore are warm and muggy. El Salvador, Belize, Honduras, and Mexico all border the nation.

PEOPLE AND CULTURE

The arithmetic and astronomy of the Mayan culture were very sophisticated. The Maya most likely invented the idea of zero and used full words and hieroglyphics to write documents.

The Maya civilization started to fragment and break apart into several tribes around the tenth century, while historians are unsure of the exact cause of the Maya Empire's downfall. It's possible that both the impacts of the drought and overcrowding affected them.

Maya women still weave vibrant fabrics and make the same kind of trade, or suit, that their foremothers wore. Native Americans make up more than half of the population. The Quiché, the biggest of the 20 Maya communities, are concentrated around Quetzaltenango, which the inhabitants refer to as Xela (SHEH-la).

TRAVEL ESSENTIALS

BEST TIME TO VISIT

The dry season, which runs from November to April, is the ideal time to visit Guatemala. The range of 23°C to 32°C is comfortable and warm.

The hills are renowned for their lovely, warm days and chilly evenings. The lowlands around Tikal are typically warm throughout the year, with highs in the mid-20s and lows in the mid-30s, with higher humidity starting in May. Nonetheless, Guatemala has a lovely climate that makes travel there possible all year round. In the major tourist areas, rainfall often occurs for a few hours each day, even during the rainy season, which runs from May to October. Only if you want to combine your vacation with some beach time in Belize do we advise avoiding traveling in September and October due to the more disruptive weather in these months.

VISA REQUIREMENTS

The following paperwork has to be gathered and submitted to the Guatemalan embassy or consulate closest to your place of residence to apply for a visa to Guatemala:

A passport that will still be valid six months after you depart from Guatemala.

One current color passport-size picture.

Form of application. Fill out the online application for Guatemala, download it, and sign it when you're done.

valid health insurance for the trip. You must have current health insurance that will pay for any bills you may incur while in Guatemala.

Evidence of accommodations. a paper demonstrating that you are staying in Guatemala. This might be a letter of invitation, a hotel reservation, a rental agreement, etc.

A letter on the cover stating why you are visiting Guatemala.

A letter of invitation from a friend or family member who resides in Guatemala. The invitation letter has to attest to your accommodation and sponsoring status in the nation.

A copy of your bank statement attesting to your stability and ability to support yourself while in Guatemala.

A record of criminal activity. The criminal record is a record provided by the law enforcement agency in your nation of origin; it serves as evidence that you pose no danger to Guatemala.

Itinerary for the flight. Your flight information, including the date and time of the trip, the name of the airline, and a ticket for the return journey, must be included in the flight itinerary document.

HEALTH AND SAFETY TIPS

1. Vaccinations and Health Precautions:

- **Vaccinations:** Ensure your routine vaccinations are up-to-date. Additionally, Hepatitis A, Typhoid, and Yellow Fever vaccinations are recommended. Consult with a travel medicine specialist ideally 4-6 weeks before your trip.

- **Altitude Sickness:** If you plan to visit high-altitude areas like Quetzaltenango or the Western Highlands, acclimate slowly to avoid altitude sickness.

- **Traveler's Diarrhea:** Be cautious with food and water. Drink bottled or purified water, avoid ice, and eat well-cooked foods.

2. Travel Insurance:

- Invest in comprehensive travel insurance that covers medical emergencies, evacuation, and trip cancellation.

3. Safety Tips:

- **Crime:** While Guatemala has made strides in reducing crime, it's wise to stay vigilant. Avoid isolated areas, don't display expensive items, and use trusted transportation services.

- **Transportation:** Use licensed taxis or reputable transportation services, especially at night.
- **Natural Hazards:** Guatemala is prone to earthquakes and volcanic activity. Familiarize yourself with safety protocols for natural disasters.

4. Road Safety:

- If you're driving, be cautious as road conditions and local driving practices can be challenging. Avoid driving at night due to reduced visibility and increased risk of criminal activity.

5. Respect Local Laws and Customs:

- Be aware of and respect local laws. Drug offenses carry strict penalties, including lengthy prison sentences.
- Respect cultural norms, especially when visiting indigenous communities or sacred sites.

6. Environmental Care:

- Practice responsible tourism. Respect wildlife, keep natural areas clean, and support eco-friendly businesses.

7. Connectivity:

- Ensure you have a means to communicate in case of emergency.

8. Learn Basic Spanish:

- Knowing basic Spanish phrases can greatly enhance your experience and help in emergencies.

9. Register with Your Embassy:

- Register with your embassy or consulate upon arrival for safety updates and assistance in case of emergency.

10. Be Prepared for the Climate:

- Guatemala's climate varies by region. Pack appropriate clothing, use sun protection in high-altitude and tropical areas, and stay hydrated.

CURRENCY AND PAYMENT METHODS

1. Currency:

- **Guatemalan Quetzal (GTQ):** The local currency is the Guatemalan Quetzal, named after the national bird. It's advisable to have some local currency on hand for small purchases, as not all places accept credit cards.

- **US Dollars:** US dollars are widely accepted, especially in tourist areas. However, smaller denominations are preferred, and you should expect a change in quetzals.

2. Exchanging Money:

- **Airports and Banks:** You can exchange currency at the airport, banks, or authorized exchange offices. Banks usually offer better rates than airport exchanges.

- **ATMs:** Widely available in cities and tourist areas, ATMs are a convenient way to withdraw quetzals. Be mindful of your surroundings when using an ATM and check for any signs of tampering.

3. Credit and Debit Cards:

- **Acceptance:** Major credit cards like Visa and MasterCard are accepted in most hotels, restaurants, and larger stores, especially in tourist areas. However, smaller establishments and rural areas may only accept cash.

- **Fees:** Be aware of potential foreign transaction fees charged by your bank or card issuer.

4. Budgeting Tips:

- **Daily Budget:** Prices in Guatemala can be lower than in many Western countries. Budgeting around 300-500 quetzales per day can cover moderate spending for meals, transportation, and entrance fees.

- **Tipping:** Tipping is customary in restaurants and for services. Around 10% is standard, but always check if service is included in the bill.

5. Bargaining:

- **Markets and Street Vendors:** Bargaining is a common practice in markets and with street vendors. It's part of the local shopping culture but always negotiated respectfully.

6. Receipts and Documentation:

- Always ask for receipts, especially when exchanging money or making significant purchases. This is important for tracking your spending and for any potential reimbursement claims.

7. Tax Refunds:

- Guatemala currently doesn't offer VAT refunds for tourists on purchases made in the country.

8. Financial Safety:

- **Avoid Carrying Large Amounts of Cash:** It's safer to carry only what you need for the day.

- **Use a Money Belt:** For added security, consider using a money belt to keep your cash and cards concealed.

9. Emergency Funds:

- Have some emergency funds or a backup credit card in case of unexpected expenses or emergencies.

10. Understanding Pricing:

- Be aware that in tourist areas, prices may be higher compared to local markets. Understanding the average cost of items can help you make informed purchases.

LANGUAGE AND COMMUNICATION

Language of Official Documentation: **1. Spanish: ** The majority of people in Guatemala speak Spanish, which is the official language of the country. It is the main language spoken in the courts, on television, and in schools.

2. Rich Linguistic Diversity: - **Indigenous Languages:** A sizable indigenous community speaks more than 20 distinct Mayan dialects in Guatemala. These include Q'eqchi', Mam, Kaqchikel, and K'iche', each with a distinct linguistic history.

Different Regions: Regional differences exist in the predominance of indigenous languages. Native languages are spoken more often than Spanish in many rural regions, particularly in the Western Highlands.

3. Acquiring Foundational Spanish Knowledge: - **Key Expressions:** Being able to communicate in basic Spanish will make your trip much more enjoyable. Basic hellos, phone numbers, and frequently asked questions may be quite helpful.

- **Courses in Language:** Many language schools in Guatemala provide intensive Spanish language lessons, making it a popular location for language learners.

4. English Usage: - **Tourist Areas:** English is often spoken in hotels, restaurants, and by tour guides in major tourist attractions and bigger cities.

Restricted to Rural Regions: Basic Spanish knowledge is useful since English competence is less widespread in rural and less popular locations.

5. Etiquette for Communication: - **Politeness:** Guatemalans often communicate formally. It is appreciated to use titles such as "Señor" or "Señora" together with courteous words.

- **Intelligent Cues:** In Guatemala, nonverbal cues and body language are important. Keeping eye contact conveys respect and attention.

6. Engaging with Native American Communities:
- **Empathy and Sensitivity:** It is crucial to treat Native Americans with respect and to take an interest in their language and culture.

Related Resources: It might be enlightening to hire guides who are fluent in both the local indigenous language and Spanish, particularly in regions where indigenous languages are the majority language.

7. Technology and Tools for Translation: - **Translation Applications:** Although smartphone translation applications may be useful in situations when language is a problem, they shouldn't be the only source of reliable communication.

- **Accessibility of WiFi:** In towns and popular tourist locations, Wi-Fi is often accessible, although, in isolated locations, the connection may be spotty.

8. Written Materials and signs: - Written materials and signs are mostly in Spanish, particularly in tourist regions. Some could even have translations into English.

9. Radio and Television: - A variety of radio stations and television channels provide programming in Spanish, and the language is used extensively in media.

10. Welcome the Linguistic Experience: - Interacting with the people in their native tongues, even if it's only by picking up a few K'iche' words or practicing your Spanish with them, may make your trip to Guatemala much more meaningful.

MAJOR DESTINATIONS

GUATEMALA CITY: THE CAPITAL

Following the earthquake that rocked Antigua in 1773, King Carlos III of Spain issued an edict in 1776 that established the capital city of Guatemala.

The biggest urban area in Central America as of right now is Guatemala City.

Luxurious hotels, inventive dining options, colorful buses, and lively nightlife are just a few of its attractions.

Zone 1: The Presidential Palace and Plaza Mayor

There are twenty-one zones in the city. The largest historic structures in the city are located in Zone 1, which encircles the expansive Plaza Mayor.

The plaza, which is among the biggest in Central America, is comparable to Mexico City's Zocalo.

Built-in 1943, the National Palace is open for tours of its exquisite chambers and the Presidential Balcony, which provides views over the plaza.

A perpetual light honors the "anonymous heroes of peace" in front of the palace.

The National Library and the 18th-century Catedral Metropolitana are two other noteworthy locations.

Zone 7: Kaminaljuyu

The Kaminaljuyu Archeological Park, located in Zone 7, three miles west of the city center, preserves more than 200 platforms and clay mounds, which are the remains of a massive Pre-Classic Maya metropolis that originally occupied a third of the valley.

Upon excavating a handful of these mounds, fifth-century adobe pyramids and a ball court were discovered.

The superb Miraflores Museum in Zone 11 is home to many of the objects uncovered in Kaminaljuyu.

Zone 10 is home to many excellent museums.

Here are two museums that showcase an amazing collection of masks, ceramics, and textiles from Guatemala: Museo Popol Vuh and Museo Ixchel.

How to Get to Guatemala City: International flights are operated out of Zone 13's La Aurora International Airport, which serves Central and North America.

For guests, this airport is the obvious place to arrive. It's just 25 miles to the west of Antigua.

There are many daily departures from Flores, the entry point to Tikal, which can be reached in less than an hour. Temperatures in Guatemala City are generally consistent, with highs in the mid-90s and lows around 70.

Light precipitation occurs from November to May. June through October sees sporadic rains and somewhat lower temperatures.

ANTIGUA: COLONIAL CHARM

La Antigua Guatemala was established on March 10, 1543, and in 1979, UNESCO designated it as a World Heritage Site. With over 500 years of history, this stunning and enchanted colonial city has a favorable environment and a breathtaking view of the Fire and Acatenango volcanoes.

Located in the Panchoy Valley, La Antigua is the third seat of the Guatemalan capital. Time seemed to have stopped in this city, imprisoned inside the fortified walls of its colonial homes, temples, and monasteries. With its cobblestone lanes, this vibrant town still boasts houses from the sixteenth century that have been renovated.

Northeast of the city, on Cerro de la Cruz, is where La Antigua Guatemala seems to be quite spectacular. Furthermore, the iconic Water Volcano is remarkable since it has seen the rise and fall of the populace. Every little element in this city adds to its splendor. Visitors are astounded by its historical landmarks and the venerable monasteries and temples that still stand as a testament to its past.

It has withstood many earthquakes, remained steady throughout time, and is beloved for its cobblestone streets, colonial homes, public monuments, folklore, and customs.

The Palace of the General Captains, the Convent and Arch of Santa Catalina, the Plaza Mayor, the Jade Museum, the Antigua Guatemala Cathedral, the University of San Carlos Museum, and the Holy Route of Brother Pedro are some of the primary tourist destinations in La Antigua. Along with traditional weavings, pottery, metallic goods, silver and gold items, traditional sweets, and cuisine, the city is also rich in handicrafts.

From Guatemala City, travel the CA-1 route, passing past the Roosevelt Causeway and San Lucas Sacatepéquez, to reach La Antigua Guatemala. The distance between Antigua and the capital city's core is forty kilometers.

The Best Activities and Attractions:

1. **Central Park, or Parque Central): Commence your discovery at Parque Central, the center of Antigua. Historic sites like the magnificent Catedral de San José and the Palacio de los Capitanes Generales are around this quaint plaza. It's a nice spot to unwind, observe people, and take in the ambience.

2. The San José Cathedral: Antigua's skyline is dominated by this majestic church built in the Baroque style. For sweeping views of the city and neighboring volcanoes, go to the roof. Inside lies the tranquil Capilla del Cristo, which is home to exquisite religious artwork. Don't miss it.

3. The Cathedral Museum of Antigua Guatemala: This museum, which is next to the cathedral, has a collection of religious items and artwork from colonial times that provide light on the religious past of the city.

4. The Arch of Santa Catalina: Once a part of the Santa Catalina convent, this bright yellow arch is one of Antigua's most recognizable images. It provides a lovely background for images and artfully frames the Agua Volcano.

5. The Church of La Merced: This remarkable church has an exquisite Baroque façade with elaborate stucco work. Inside are noteworthy exhibits of holy treasures and a magnificently adorned altar.

6. The Church in San Francisco: Explore the largely damaged remnants of this old church and convent caused by earthquakes. The bell tower and lovely garden provide amazing city views.

7. **House of Ancient Tejido Museum:** Visit this museum to learn about the craft of traditional Guatemalan weaving. See expert weavers at work and discover the elaborate designs and methods they use.

8. **Market Purchasing:** The marketplaces in Antigua are a veritable gold mine of regional fabrics, crafts, and mementos. A large assortment of handcrafted items may be found in the Mercado de Artesanías.

9. Tours of Coffee:** Coffee is a specialty of Guatemala, and Antigua is an excellent site to learn about the production of coffee. Savor some of the best coffee in the world by going on a guided tour of a nearby coffee farm.

10. Hiking a Volcano: Volcanoes encircle Antigua; intrepid visitors might trek Pacaya, Acatenango, or Fuego. Each provides a different trekking experience as well as the chance to see active volcanoes.

11. **Workshops on Chocolate Making:** Learn the techniques used to make chocolate in Guatemala. Take part in classes where you may make your chocolate bars and ground your cocoa beans.

LAKE ATITLÁN: NATURAL BEAUTY

The Guatemalan highlands are home to Lake Atitlán, which is well known for its stunning scenery and diverse culture. With a depth of around 340 meters, this volcanic lake is the deepest in Central America and is surrounded by the three magnificent volcanoes Atitlán, Tolimán, and San Pedro.

A significant volcanic explosion that took place more than 84,000 years ago left a crater that gradually filled with water, giving rise to the lake. Steep hills and ancient Mayan settlements, where the local languages and customs are preserved, define the surrounding terrain. There are several Maya villages in the region, each with its distinct languages, clothes, and rituals.

In addition to being a natural beauty, Lake Atitlan serves as a major destination for adventure travel and ecotourism. Along with kayaking, hiking, and paragliding, the area allows visitors to see local markets and coffee farms. The surroundings of the lake are also home to a variety of animal and plant species, which increases the lake's ecological value.

The constantly shifting look of Lake Atitlan is among its most remarkable features. The water's color and texture are often changed by the interaction of light, weather, and volcanic activity, creating a visually striking sight. This, together with the ancient Maya civilization, makes the lake a wellspring of inspiration for authors and artists worldwide.

Lake Atitlán has natural beauty, yet it also has environmental problems. The health of the lake and the lives of the populations who rely on it are threatened by problems including pollution, deforestation, and the effects of climate change. To protect this natural gem for future generations, local and international organizations are working on conservation projects.

Known as one of the world's most beautiful lakes, Lake Atitlan is a popular tourist attraction in Guatemala. Adventure activities, boat trips between towns, and wandering through the several authentic Mayan villages around Lake Atitlan are all available to visitors.

In addition to all the delights this lake has to offer, the region around Lake Atitlan is the greatest spot to get fully immersed in the indigenous Mayan culture. There is a Mayan language unique to each town around the lake. Depending on their beliefs and culture, people dress in traditional ways. You'll be itching to return to Guatemala after seeing this lovely location in the country's Western Highlands!

Activities around Lake Atitlan

Exploring Lake Atitlan

Lake Atitlan, which is protected by the volcanoes San Pedro, Atitlan, and Toliman, is a wonderful blend of natural beauty, a serene setting, and a wealth of Mayan culture.

There are plenty of things available at Lake Atitlan to suit every taste and keep you occupied while there. Take a coffee or bird-watching excursion, trek the surrounding highlands and volcanoes, or learn how to weave traditional fabrics. If you like water activities, you may go diving, kayaking, jet skiing, or, for a rush of excitement, you can leap from a 7-meter (23-foot) platform at San Marcos La Laguna to cool down. Lake Atitlan serves as a jumping off place for amazing adventures!

Excursions from Lake Atitlan to other nearby locations in Chichicastenango

Come explore this ethereal village that is close to Lake Atitlan. Because the people there are so devout to their faith, it's quite probable that you may see a Mayan rite while you're there. The main draw in this town is the market in Chichi. A vibrant market is set up every

Thursday and Sunday to welcome tourists from all around the globe.

Quetzaltenango

Lake Atitlan is three hours distant from Guatemala's second-biggest metropolis. Quetzaltenango, surrounded by hills and mountains, provides a range of outdoor activities to keep you in touch with the natural world.

The Totonicapan

Totonicapan, about an hour's drive from Lake Atitlan, is well-known for housing one of Guatemala's most remarkable churches. San Andres Xecul is a church that honors both its Christian tradition and the Mayan origins of its community.

Shopping at Lake Atitlan

The main thoroughfare in Panajachel for souvenir shopping of all kinds is Calle Santander. These kinds of trinkets may be found on the commercial streets of almost every community around Lake Atitlan. Since these streets are often found where the boats unload, finding them is simple.

Towns around Lake Atitlan

Panajachel Panajachel is the starting point for exploring the several indigenous settlements around Lake Atitlan. This village is situated within the magnificent backdrop of the San Pedro, Toliman, and Atitlan volcanoes. Panajachel also acts as a starting point for visiting the twelve native communities that surround Lake Atitlan.

Palopo, Santa Catarina

A vibrant town you should visit at least once in your lifetime! Santa Catarina Palopo is an intriguing blend of contemporary and old, while yet maintaining its traditions. In addition, it is home to Casa Palopó, one of the most exquisite hotels in the nation—a warm spot with a distinct aesthetic.

La Laguna San Marcos

San Marcos La Laguna, also referred to as the "hippie town" of Lake Atitlan, is the ideal location for unwinding and meditation. There's a good concentration of vegetarian and vegan eateries and high-quality lodging nearby. It also has the Cerro Tzankujil Natural Reserve, which is well-known for its seven-meter-tall (23-foot) jumping trampoline. Ideal for dipping into Lake Atitlan's enchanted waters!

La Laguna, San Juan

Both San Juan La Laguna's population and tourism are increasing. It is well-known for its organically colored textiles, healing herbs, regional artists, spirituality, and the outdoors. When you visit this strange community, San Juan La Laguna will provide you with an experience that is distinct and unusual.

Laguna de San Pedro

The town of San Pedro La Laguna receives the most tourists in Lake Atitlan. Because of its wonderful surroundings, it has a large reputation among backpackers and a worldwide social scene. There are a lot of eateries, bars, and travel agencies in one area, providing you with lots of entertainment options.

Atitlan, Santiago

The cultural hub of Lake Atitlan is Santiago Atitlan. The earliest people to live by the Lake did so here. They maintain their customs in their most unadulterated form because of this. If you can, try to visit Santiago Atitlan on a Sunday when almost all of the native women will be dressed in their traditional finest attire since it is part of their customs. Santiago is especially well-known for its devotion to Maximon, commonly known as The Big Grandpa, a saint that was originally established by Mayan priests.

TIKAL: ANCIENT MAYAN RUINS

One of the most important Maya archeological sites is Tikal, which is tucked away in the northern Guatemalan woods. This once-thriving metropolis, which is recognized as a UNESCO World Heritage Site, goes back to the 4th century BC and peaked between 200 and 900 AD.

The magnificent architectural complex known as the Great Plaza is located in the center of Tikal. The Temple of the Great Jaguar (Temple I) and the Temple of the Masks (Temple II), which border the plaza, are marvels for tourists to see. Temple I, standing more than 47 meters tall and renowned for its imposing height and steep stairs, is a well-known representation of Tikal. Slightly shorter, Temple II's peak provides an amazing view of the Great Plaza.

Tikal's vast complex has a plethora of buildings, including palaces, temples, ceremonial platforms, and ball courts, in addition to the Great Plaza. The highest pre-Columbian building in the Americas, Temple IV, stands out amid them all and provides sweeping vistas of the surrounding forest with other temples visible through the canopy.

It's an immersive experience to visit Tikal. The Tikal National Park, a huge tract of tropical rainforest that is home to an amazing variety of animals, including coatis, spider monkeys, howler monkeys, and hundreds of bird species, envelops the site. Early in the morning, as the mist lifts and the temples appear, the forest comes alive with the sounds of nature.

Guided tours are among the tourist activities that provide information about the history, culture, and architecture of the pre-Columbian Maya. Hiking routes allow for a more thorough examination of the site as they wind through the forest, linking several complexes and lesser-known remains. There are plenty of possibilities to see animals and birds in the nearby rainforest for those who like doing such activities.

Another well-liked activity is photography, with the dawn and sunset excursions being especially popular because of the stunning vistas and distinctive play of light and shadow on the ancient ruins.

It's best to spend a whole day touring Tikal to truly appreciate the sight. Many tourists base themselves in the adjacent town of Flores, where lodging is available. Set against the backdrop of a lush, breathing jungle, Tikal is more than simply a historical site—it's a voyage into the heart of an ancient society. It's a location where nature and history meet, providing an experience that will never be forgotten.

CHICHICASTENANGO: MARKET AND CULTURE

Chichicastenango, sometimes known as "Chichi," is a bustling town in the Guatemalan highlands that is well-known for its lively market and rich indigenous culture. Located around 140 kilometers northwest of Guatemala City, this hamlet is a must-see for anybody looking for a genuine look into the customs and way of life of the Maya people of Guatemala?

The Marketplace:

Chichicastenango's vibrant market, which takes place on Thursdays and Sundays, is its hub. It's one of Central America's biggest and busiest indigenous marketplaces. There is an abundance of things available at the stalls, ranging from fresh vegetables and local delicacies to hand-woven fabrics, traditional masks, ceramics, and wood sculptures. The market offers a cultural experience in addition to being a place to buy. In addition to interacting with local artists and enjoying the food, tourists may see how the Maya people in the area dress traditionally.

Santo Tomás Church:

Located on the east side of the market square, this 400-year-old church combines Maya and Catholic religious customs. The church steps were formerly part of a pre-Columbian temple, and Maya priests still carry out ceremonies and light incense there. Inside, it's a special place for spirituality because of the combination of Catholic and native Maya religious images.

Abaj Pascual:

The hilltop temple to the Maya soil god, Pascual Abaj, is only a short stroll from the town center. The location is utilized for customary Maya rites and rituals. Experiencing the live Maya culture and spirituality in this location is quite remarkable.

Museo Ceremonial de Máscaras:

The intriguing collection of traditional masks used in Maya rites and dances is on display at this museum. The vibrant masks, which often feature animals, historical people, or fantastical creatures, provide light on the rich mythology of the area.

Chichicastenango Cemetery:

The town's cemetery embodies the Maya beliefs about life and death and is a brilliant display of colors. The vividly painted mausoleums and graves provide a distinctive viewpoint on the regional traditions related to dying and remembering.

Activities and Advice: - **Shopping:** For those wishing to buy genuine handmade trinkets, the market is a veritable delight. It's normal to haggle, so don't be afraid to discuss pricing.

- **Cultural Immersion:** Talk to regional producers and craftspeople. A lot of people like telling tales about their trades.

Photography: Chichicastenango has a wealth of photo possibilities; but, as with any place, get permission before taking pictures of the locals, particularly amid religious festivities.

- **Local Cuisine:** Visit the market or nearby restaurants to sample regional cuisines like tamales or pepián.

- **Overnight Stay:** After the market closes and the visitors go, consider staying the night in Chichicastenango to take in the atmosphere of the town.

OUTDOOR ADVENTURES

HIKING AND TREKKING ROUTES

Every hiking fan will adore Guatemala's very unique hiking experiences, which range from climbing the tallest volcano in Central America to going through the forest to unexplored Mayan sites. I have compiled a list of some of the top treks in Guatemala that you shouldn't miss, even if there are far too many to include them all!

Lake Atitlan - Xela

Unquestionably one of the greatest multi-day walks in Guatemala is from Xela to Lake Atitlan. This three-day hike will take you from Quetzaltenango, often known as Xela, the second-biggest city in Guatemala, to the well-liked tourist attraction, Lake Atitlan. Even if there would be no adventure in taking a speedier and bumpier chicken bus to Lake Atitlan! As an alternative, the trip from Xela to Lake Atitlan will take you through the stunning Western Highlands of Guatemala, where you will cross river valleys, ascend steep cornfields, and discover secluded indigenous towns. Upon reaching the summit of the trek, you will be treated to breathtaking vistas of Lake

Atitlan and other nearby volcanoes. Additionally, if you reserve a guided trek, you'll often spend the night in a nearby homestay, which offers a great dinner prepared by the host and a warm shower—two amenities that are very helpful after a strenuous day of hiking.

Volcán Tajumulco

Volcán Tajumulco is the ideal climb for those who want to summit all of the mountains! The tallest peak in all of Central America, Volcán Tajumulco, rises to a formidable 4,203 meters.

Although Tajumulco's height may appear daunting on paper, don't let that deter you—this is a rather modest trek that is doable for anybody with a respectable degree of fitness. The height is Volcán Tajumulco's largest obstacle. To acclimate, I would suggest that you stay a few days in the neighboring city of Quetzaltenango (Xela). While a day journey to Volcán Tajumulco is feasible, it is best to take two days to climb it, spend the night on the volcano, and see the stunning sunrise the following morning.

Hiking Volcán Tajumulco for two days will take you via little agricultural communities and pine woods before arriving at the top of Central America's largest volcano.

The name Volcán Tajumulco, which means "above the clouds" in the native Mayan tongue, is quite fitting given the breathtaking vistas that await you upon reaching the peak, spanning over Guatemala and neighboring Mexico. You may even view the Pacific Ocean from the summit if the weather is cooperative.

Acatenango Volcano

Climbing Volcán Acatenango, perhaps the most well-liked trek in Guatemala, is an amazing experience that you just must have when visiting Antigua. Hiking up Volcán Acatenango may be quite difficult and can provide a challenge to the most experienced hikers, but the journey to the top is well worth it. This popular walk is sometimes underestimated. Although the 3,976-meter peak of Acatenango is reached by hiking through cloud forests, the breathtaking view of Volcán de Fuego, its neighbor, is what really sets this walk out as one of the greatest in Guatemala.

Hiking to the peak of Acatenango will reward you with breathtaking views of Fuego, one of Guatemala's most active volcanoes, which may erupt as often as once every fifteen to twenty minutes. Depending on your trip, if you're feeling daring, you may take an extra climb to Volcán de Fuego, which will give you a far better look at the amazing eruptions. For this climb, make sure you pack warm clothes and a decent jacket since the peak may become chilly in the early morning.

El Mirador Forest Trek

Want to explore undiscovered Mayan ruins tucked away in the heart of the Guatemalan jungle? Bring out your inner Indiana Jones. If so, then the El Mirador Jungle Trek is the best walk you can undertake in Guatemala! With the ultimate objective of visiting the largest Mayan site in all of Central America, this five to six-day walk will take you through the deep Guatemalan rainforest, home to a variety of animals, including the region's howler monkeys. The world's biggest pyramid in terms of volume, the Danta Pyramid, is located inside these magnificent Mayan ruins. The El Mirador jungle journey, which is only accessible by trekking or helicopter, is a very unique experience for any outdoor lover or history buff.

Some information to bear in mind: Although Guatemala is a fairly safe country to visit and has a thriving tourist industry, you should always be alert and aware of your surroundings when traveling around the nation. Make sure you investigate the locations you will be visiting before your trip since certain parts of the nation are seen to be less secure than others.

In Guatemala, most people speak Spanish, with very few people knowing English. You should familiarize yourself with some of the fundamentals before your journey. You may study the fundamentals of Spanish for your trip with the aid of many free internet resources.

You could experience some impacts from the high altitude of many treks in Guatemala. Try to spend some time at altitude and acclimate before taking on these hikes.

Although you may trek most of the year-round, the rainy season runs from May to October, so if you want to come during these months, bring rain gear.

Make sure your hiking pack fits comfortably. Look at Paddy Pallin's hiking backpack.

VOLCANO EXPLORATION

Pacaya

Due to the several active volcanoes in the country, hikers and volcano enthusiasts often visit Guatemala. The Pacaya volcano, which lies just 25 km (15 miles) south of Guatemala City, is perhaps the country's most well-known volcano. Since 1965, this volcano, which is among the most active in Central America, has not stopped erupting.

Fuego

The Fuego volcano, which is about 30 kilometers (18 miles) from Antigua, a well-liked tourist destination in Guatemala, is another well-known volcano. One of the most active volcanoes in Central America is the Fuego volcano, which is renowned for its breathtaking explosions that are visible for kilometers around. Because it provides a strenuous trek to the peak, hikers are also drawn to the volcano.

Santa Maria

Hikers and volcano enthusiasts also often visit the Santa Maria volcano. One of the most active volcanoes in Central America, it is situated close to the Mexican border in the western portion of the nation. Moreover, the Santa Maria volcano is well-known for its breathtaking eruptions, which are visible for kilometers around. Because it provides a strenuous trek to the peak, hikers are also drawn to the volcano.

Acatenango

Another well-liked location for hikers and volcano aficionados is the Acatenango volcano. One of Central

America's most active volcanoes, it is close to the city of Antigua. Moreover, the Acatenango volcano is well-known for its breathtaking eruptions, which are visible for kilometers around. Because it provides a strenuous trek to the peak, hikers are also drawn to the volcano.

Atitlan

Hikers and volcano lovers also often visit the Atitlan volcano. One of Central America's most active volcanoes, it is close to the city of Antigua. Moreover, the Atitlan volcano is well-known for its breathtaking eruptions, which are visible for kilometers around. Because it provides a strenuous trek to the peak, hikers are also drawn to the volcano.

A few of these volcanoes are still active, and their eruptions have the potential to endanger hikers and tourists as well as harm neighboring populations. Hiking with reliable organizations and local guides who have connections to the government is crucial.

ACTIVITIES AT LAKE ATITLÁN

Overlook Lake Atitlan, parachute

Imagine yourself flying over Lake Atitlan by a thousand feet. Getting thermals? Sipping in a breathtaking vista tinged with peril?

Though it's on my list of things to do, I haven't yet taken a paragliding tour and thrown myself from a cliff. When I'm by the lakeside, I often encounter paragliders. High above the lake, they emerge on the ridge, turn, and drift on the wind like pollen. It seems to be an amazing and magnificent journey.

Check out Real World Paragliding if you want to go paragliding in Lake Atitlan. This business has a long history of operation in Panajachel. They have a solid reputation, excellent equipment, and a group of skilled pilots who have parachuted in the Himalayas, Austria, and Italy.

Renting a jet ski is an additional exciting sport that will have you yelling and heart racing. In the morning, the lake is at its smoothest. Hooting and yelling and enjoying the fun of your life, you may bomb over the waves. It was so much fun when my brother took me out on a jet ski at Lake Atitlan. It is highly recommended by me.

If you like doing daring things, you may also try flying a flyboard. You can do a ton of wacky things with this quirky gizmo both above and below the sea. I find flyboarding to be very difficult, yet according to Atlantic Flyboard, most users can start flying in the first five minutes and learn the fundamentals in only twenty.

Through a steep ravine, zipline

Great ziplining may be found at Lake Atitlan. In actuality, the area around the lake is home to Guatemala's longest and tallest zip lines. This exercise will raise your heart rate!

The Reserva Natural de Atitlán is home to the longest zipline. The ability to ride a bicycle over a zipline is included in their Ultra and X-treme zipline packages. They have a 2,822-foot-long zipline. Yes. Whoa.

Take an ATV tour to blend culture and revs.

ATV trips from Panajachel are a great option if you want to mix some action with a cultural excursion. This enjoyable excursion brings guests to one of Panajachel's top beaches as well as the communities of San Antonio and Santa Catarina Palopó. You will get to speed up and down the winding road to Santa Catarina and then slide on dirt to reach San Antonio throughout the trip. The trip begins at 9:00 am, so there should be plenty of lake views. Simoone Tours is in charge of this excursion. Their guides are well-informed, amiable, and fluent in both Spanish and English.

Savor the curves when on a motorcycle excursion

A motorbike excursion is another fantastic Lake Atitlan adventure activity. There are TONS of amazing motorbike routes around Lake Atitlan. Enjoy some amazing vistas, lean into turns, ride up and down hills, and feel a sense of freedom and exhilaration.

BIKING TRAILS

1. **Antigua Trails:**

- Located around the historic city of Antigua, these trails offer a mix of cobblestone city streets and rural dirt paths. Riders can explore coffee plantations, and local villages, and enjoy views of the surrounding volcanoes. The trails around Antigua cater to all levels, with options for easy rides as well as more challenging ascents towards the volcanoes.

2. **Lake Atitlán Trails:**

- The area around Lake Atitlán is known for its stunning beauty and challenging mountain biking trails. The paths take riders through traditional Mayan villages, and coffee fields, and offer panoramic views of the lake and its volcanic surroundings. The trails here can be quite steep and rocky, making them more suitable for intermediate to advanced riders.

3. **El Zur Mountain Bike Park:**

- Located near Guatemala City, El Zur is a dedicated mountain bike park. It features a variety of trails, including downhill and cross-country routes. The park is designed for different skill levels, offering everything from smooth, flowy trails to more technical and steep descents.

4. **Alta Verapaz Trails:**

- For those looking to explore the lush, green landscapes of Guatemala, the Alta Verapaz region offers trails through dense rainforests leading to hidden waterfalls and caves. The terrain here is generally more suited to intermediate and advanced cyclists, due to its natural obstacles and muddy conditions during the rainy season.

5. **Volcano Pacaya:**

- For an unforgettable experience, the trails around Volcano Pacaya offer a unique blend of adventure and natural beauty. The ride involves challenging lava fields and sandy trails, with the reward of stunning views of the active volcano. This trail is recommended for more experienced bikers due to the rough and uneven terrain.

6. **Mayan Cross-Country Journey:**

- This is a long-distance trail that takes riders on a journey through various Mayan archaeological sites and traditional villages. The trail traverses diverse landscapes, including jungle paths and hilly terrains, making it an excellent choice for those looking for a multi-day biking adventure.

7. **Ixil Triangle Trails:**

- Located in the Cuchumatanes mountains, the Ixil Triangle offers a network of trails connecting the towns of Nebaj, Chajul, and Cotzal. This area is less traveled, providing a more authentic experience of rural Guatemala with breathtaking mountain views.

Tips for Biking in Guatemala:

- **Hire a Local Guide:** For the best experience and to ensure safety, consider hiring a local guide, especially for the more challenging trails.
- **Check Equipment:** Ensure your bike and equipment are in good condition. Many trails in Guatemala are remote and have limited access to repair shops.
- **Stay Hydrated:** The climate can be hot and humid, especially in the rainforest regions, so carry plenty of water.

CULTURAL EXPERIENCES

MAYAN HERITAGE SITES

1. **Tikal:**

- Tikal, a UNESCO World Heritage Site, is one of the largest and most important Mayan archaeological sites. Located in the Petén Basin, it dates back to the 4th century BC. This ancient city features towering pyramids, plazas, and temples such as the Temple of the Great Jaguar and Temple IV, the tallest pre-Columbian structure in the

Americas. The surrounding rainforest adds to its mystical allure and is home to a diverse range of wildlife.

2. **Yaxhá:**

- Situated between the lagoons of Yaxhá and Sacnab, Yaxhá offers a serene setting. This lesser-known site features over 500 structures, including pyramid temples, ball courts, and an impressive complex of astronomical significance. The view of the sunset from the top of the main pyramid is breathtaking.

3. **Quiriguá:**

- Located in the southeastern region of Guatemala, Quiriguá is famous for its well-preserved stelae and zoomorphic sculptures. It's a relatively smaller site but holds significant historical importance due to its intricately carved stelae, which depict various Mayan rulers and provide insights into Mayan history and mythology.

4. **Aguateca:**

- Aguateca is unique for its setting on a cliff overlooking the Petexbatún Lagoon. This site is known for its well-preserved defensive walls and structures, providing insights into the military aspects of Mayan civilization. The natural beauty surrounding Aguateca enhances the experience of visiting this archaeological site.

5. **El Mirador:**

- El Mirador is one of the most ancient Mayan cities, known for its massive size and monumental architecture, including the largest pyramid by volume in the world, La Danta. Located in a remote area of the Guatemalan jungle, it offers an adventurous journey for visitors, often involving a multi-day trek.

6. **Iximché:**

- Situated in the Western Highlands near Tecpán, Iximché was the capital of the Kaqchikel Maya kingdom. The site features a series of plazas surrounded by palaces and temples. It's easily accessible and offers a glimpse into the post-classic period of Mayan civilization.

7. **Takalik Abaj:**

- This site is known for its unique blend of Olmec and Maya features. Located in the southwestern region of Guatemala, Takalik Abaj has a series of terraces, sculptures, and altars. Its Olmec influences provide a unique perspective on the cultural exchange between different Mesoamerican civilizations.

FESTIVALS AND CELEBRATIONS

People from Guatemala have a unique flair for large-scale celebrations.

Excessive spectacle contrasted with real demonstrations of faith, remembrance, and happiness define these festivities.

Religious customs, both Catholic and Maya, constitute the foundation of several regional and municipal celebrations as well as national holidays.

Cofradias: In the majority of towns, religious symbols are cared for and holiday festivities are organized by elected committees called cofradias.

Even the wildest holiday celebrations are influenced by the Franciscan missionaries of the sixteenth century, who are the ancestors of several of these organizations.

Among our favorite occasions are: carnival

The week before Lent, in February, is when the Carnival festival is observed.

Compared to Brazilian carnivals, the Guatemalan carnival is much more kid-friendly and mild.

The two most notable examples are located in Livingston, a city on the Caribbean coast, and the southwest near Retalhuleu.

Santa Semana, or Holy Week

The weeklong commemoration of Christian Holy Week, known as Semana Santa, is the most well-known holiday in all of Guatemala.

It's possible to argue that Antigua's celebrations are the best in Latin America.

Church floors and city sidewalks are covered with vibrantly colored carpets made of sawdust and flower petals, known as alfombras.

Good Friday and Palm Sunday

There are processions every day, but on Palm Sunday and Good Friday, the biggest are staged.

On or after the equinox of March 21st, Easter is observed on the first Sunday after the full moon; Semana Santa may occur at any time between late March and mid-April.

During Holy Week, most of Antigua's finest hotels have a minimum stay of four nights. Many have months-long waitlists.

Day of Ascension, or Jueves de Ascensión

Ascension Day is commemorated annually on May 9th at Lake Chicabal, a highland crater lake that is important to the Mam Maya.

There will be prayers, flowers, and traditional music at this lakeside celebration of Guatemalan culture.

Santiago Fiesta (Antigua Fair)

In Guatemala, town fairs are a long-standing custom, with the majority taking place on the day of the town's patron saint.

The feast of Santiago, or Saint James, is held in Antigua on July 25.

There are carnival rides, music, traditional dance, and processions at this Guatemalan celebration.

The National Folkloric Festival of Guatemala, or Fiesta Nacional Indigena

Coban celebrates its annual Rabin Ajau festival on July 27.

Indigenous communities from all around Guatemala come together for this event to perform traditional dances and songs from their ancestors.

The main event of the celebration is a pageant where Maya women vie to be crowned Queen.

The main criterion used to evaluate contestants is their adherence to Maya traditions and beliefs.

The Day of Our Lady of Assumption, or Fiesta de la Virgen de la Asunción

Guatemala City's patron saint, the Virgin of the Assumption, is celebrated on August 15.

All over the nation, there are celebrations, fairs, and parades during this holiday.

Guatemala City is the site of the biggest of these events.

The cofradia, or lay Roman Catholics, of the Lady of the Assumption walk through the streets of Sololá, Atitlan, carrying her image to the church on their shoulders.

The peaceful separation of Guatemala from Spain in 1821 is celebrated on September 15th as Dia de la Independencia, or Independence Day.

In the weeks before the celebration of Guatemalan independence, buses and buildings are decked up in patriotic blue and white decorations.

The nation also has several military parades during this period. There are dances, fiestas, local fairs, and fireworks on the actual day of celebration.

One of the biggest celebrations celebrated in Quetzaltenango is Independence Day.

Day of the Saints, or Dia de Los Santos

All Saints Day is observed on November 1st in Guatemala.

Families get together at this joyful time to visit and decorate family graves as a way of showing their respect for departed family members.

Kites are flown at these Guatemalan holidays as a symbolic attempt to reach the afterlife.

At Santiago Sacatepéquez, a little village in the highlands, tradition assumes mythical dimensions.

Santo Tomas Fiesta (Chichicastenango Fair)

Chichicastenango's town fair takes place from December 14 until December 21.

Young men put their courage and strength to the test during this festival by climbing the Palo Volador, a pole. They ride ropes to the top and then spin back down to Earth.

The celebration ambiance is enhanced with nativity displays, handcrafted Christmas decorations, and posadas, which are processions.

Adieu ao Nuevo (Eve of the New Year)

Guatemalans celebrate New Year's Eve with great zeal.

Wearing new clothing is a symbol of riches and good fortune.

All night-long celebrations ensue, with impromptu dances and music filling the air. Fireworks are very important and used extensively.

TRADITIONAL CUISINE

Even though the country's vibrant colonial architecture, breathtaking scenery, and welcoming people draw most tourists, Guatemala's underappreciated food is yet another excellent incentive to make travel plans there. Typical Guatemalan cuisine is diverse and reflects the different populations who have called the nation home throughout its history, from colonial Spaniards to direct descendants of Afro-Indigenous communities. It combines a blend of Spanish, Afro-Caribbean, and Indigenous influences.

Despite sharing several foods with its neighbors in Central America, such as tortillas, tamales, and tostones, Guatemalan cuisine is unique. The main ingredients in most dishes are meat (pork, beef, and chicken), but peppers, chiles, and even chocolate are needed to provide flavor punch. You can also bet that your meal will be served with a basket of freshly prepared tortillas that are warm.

1. Pepián de pollo, or stewed chicken
Where to give it a go: Most Guatemalan restaurants that serve supper serve pepián, and the Cuscun culinary school in Antigua, Guatemala offers classes on how to prepare it. The national food of Guatemala is pepián, which both residents and visitors will gush over. From its modest origins as a food eaten during Mayan festivities, it has seen several modifications. Traditionally, it is served as a stew over rice with tortillas on the side. Pork and beef versions are also available for those wishing to add some spiciness to the traditional dish, even though the chicken version is perhaps the most well-liked. To prepare the meal, a complex taste profile is built by roasting a

combination of red and black chiles, sesame seeds, cilantro, tomatoes, and tomatillos separately. The roasted ingredients are then mixed into the well-loved creamy stew. When I had the chance to sample handmade pepián in Antigua, I was pleasantly surprised by how flavorful it was, with the chicken taking center stage along with soft potatoes and carrots.

2. Stuffed chili peppers, or chiles rellenos

La Fonda de la Calle Real in Antigua, Guatemala is the place to sample it.

Bell peppers filled with a combination of pork and vegetables and served over a bed of red sauce made from tomatoes are called chile rellenos, and they are usually released during family get-togethers and festivities. This meal is also popular in Mexico, where it's usually filled with jalapeño peppers instead of bell peppers with a cheese combination.

3. Jocón, a green sauce-based stew of chicken.

Where to try it: Green onions, green tomatoes, or tomatillos, green peppers, chives, cilantro, and celery are the components of this well-known green-coloured chicken stew (Arrin Coan, many places in Guatemala City and Antigua). West Guatemala's Huehuetenango area is the birthplace of jocón, a classic Mayan meal that dates back to the 1500s.

4. Soupe Kak Ik (turkey)

Where to sample it: Coban, Guatemala's El Peñascal

"Red and spicy" is an exact translation of the rich, spicy turkey soup known as kak'ik, another typical Mayan cuisine. The precise list of ingredients varies somewhat depending on the part of Guatemala the chef is from, but it always contains turkey, tomatoes, and chiles—the last of which gives it its iconic crimson hue, said to symbolize the blood spilt in the customary religious rites of the era.

5. Shredded beef stew, or hilachas

Where to sample it: Antigua and Guatemala City's 7 Caldos

This classic stew is usually served over rice and has lean shredded beef, potatoes, and carrots. The tomato-based broth has a hint of spiciness. Hilachas, which means "rags," are also popular across Central America, with each nation having its unique take on the dish.

6. Guatemalan customary breakfast, or desayuno tradicional

Where to give it a go: Served from the morning menus of most restaurants

This dish, a traditional breakfast in Guatemala, is high in protein and usually consists of eggs (fried or scrambled), sweet plantains, black beans, avocado, tomatoes, and a small portion of queso fresco, or fresh white cheese, with tortillas on the side. I would often have the breakfast plate with scrambled eggs and drink it with a cup of tea when I was traveling. It adds a little spice to the meal, so I soon learned to ask for hot chile sauce on the side.

7. Curried pork stew, or revolvedo

Try it at El Adobe, Antigua.

Revolcado, a dish that combines Spanish and indigenous cuisines, is popular across Central America. After three to four hours of boiling, the pig's head, liver, and intestines are combined with tomatoes, bell peppers, onions, garlic, and annatto—a spice recognized for its vivid red hue—to form a stew.

Shucos, or street-side hot dogs

Where to give it a go: Shucos, a street food staple in Guatemala, are often provided as a fast and simple meal at any street food market, such as Mercado Central (Guatemala City) and La Merced (Antigua). The moniker "dirties" refers to this. Though shucos are wrapped on toasted bread and topped with guacamole, cabbage, chorizo, pico de gallo, and whatever other toppings the late-night diner is in the mood for, any resemblance to the American hot dog ends at the beef sausage.

9. A platter of Guatemalan steak known as churrasco Guatemalteco

Where to give it a go: Served from the supper menus of most restaurants

Usually served for lunch or supper, this hearty steak plate comes with a churrasco, which is a grilled or barbecued beef cut. Rice, beans, sweet plantains, and guacamole on the side are often also included on the platter.

LOCAL CRAFTS AND SHOPPING

Handicrafts from Guatemala: A Cultural Tapestry

Handcrafted goods from Guatemala are more than simply decorative items; they represent a window into the rich cultural fabric of the nation. These age-old crafts, which have been handed down through the years, capture the essence of Guatemala and its indigenous people. Let's explore the wide variety of handicrafts that comprise this colorful tapestry.

Textiles: From colorful embroidery to sophisticated weavings

Guatemalan culture places a great value on textiles. Weaving has been a centuries-old craft with strong roots in Mayan customs. Using ancient backstrap looms, skilled weavers painstakingly produce vivid motifs and complex patterns. Guatemalan textiles are a kaleidoscope of colors and tales, ranging from exquisite huipiles (woven blouses) to colorful cortes (skirts) and warm ponchos.

Pottery: The skill of forming clay into exquisite ceramic objects

Pottery has a lengthy history in Guatemala, going back to pre-Columbian times. The many ceramic types seen in different parts of the nation have been impacted by the country's diverse terrain. Guatemalan pottery displays both beautiful and useful art styles, ranging from the polished ceramics of the Pacific coast to the rustic pottery of the highlands. Guatemala produces beautiful pottery, some examples of which include jars, figures, masks, and vases.

Woodworking: Dexterous engraving and artistry
Another highly respected trade in Guatemala is woodworking. Craftspeople expertly sculpt elaborate patterns and forms out of various wood species. Guatemalans are skilled woodworkers who create intricate sculptures and masks that portray Mayan mythology as well as exquisite furniture and cutlery. Every item is evidence of the artistry and skill of Guatemalan craftspeople.
Jewelry: Items of ornamentation inspired by Mayan customs

Guatemalan jewelry is a symbol of the nation's cultural past and is much more than simply ornaments. Mayan mythology is often incorporated into traditional jewelry designs via symbols and patterns. Because jade was formerly thought to be a holy stone by the Mayans, it has a unique position in Guatemalan jewelry. Guatemalan jewelry is a real representation of the artistic talent of the nation, ranging from jade jewelry to elaborately beaded masterpieces and silver adornments.

Leatherwork: Precision-crafted items created by hand
The art of leatherworking blends style and practicality. Leather products made by Guatemalan craftsmen include belts, accessories, and fashionable bags and handbags. Every piece is painstakingly made by hand and sewn by hand. The skill and attention to detail shown by Guatemalan leather workers is impressive.

Markets in Guatemala You Must Visit
Shopping in Guatemala should take place in the vibrant marketplaces. Immerse yourself in the customs and culture of the area by visiting these lively centers, which

provide a wide selection of handmade gifts. Let's investigate a few of the nation's most well-known marketplaces.

Market of Handicrafts, Guatemala City

The biggest artisan market in Guatemala City is called Mercado de Artesanías. A wide variety of handicrafts and mementos from around the nation may be found here. For those looking for genuine Guatemalan handcrafts, this market is a veritable gold mine, offering everything from exquisitely woven fabrics to hand-painted ceramics and distinctive jewelry.

Chichicastenango Market

Nestled amid Guatemala's hills, the Chichicastenango Market is an exquisite sensory experience. This market is well known for its lively ambiance and vivid colors. Vibrant vegetables, handcrafted items from local artisans, and traditional fabrics are all available as you meander around the confined aisles. Remember to haggle with the amiable sellers to get the greatest prices!

Market at Panajachel

The Panajachel Market, tucked away on Lake Atitlan's shoreline, provides a unique shopping experience among breathtakingly beautiful surroundings. With an extensive selection of paintings, fabrics, and handmade objects on exhibit, this market is a sanctuary for art fans. Enjoy a leisurely walk around the market, take in the lively ambiance, and choose the ideal item to bring home.

Market Sololá

Go to the Sololá Market for a genuine indigenous market experience. Situated in Sololá, a village in the highlands, this market serves as a center for the nearby Mayan settlements. A wide selection of locally produced vegetables, traditional apparel, and handcrafted textiles may be found here. Your attention will be captured by the fabrics' rich patterns and vivid hues.

Market in Antigua

The local market in Antigua, a colonial city, offers a mix of traditional and modern crafts. A wealth of one-of-a-kind handicrafts, including jewelry, paintings, ceramics and textiles, may be found in the Antigua Market. Explore the colorful booths, strike up a conversation with the craftspeople, and locate that unique keepsake to remember your trip to Antigua.

WILDLIFE AND NATURE

NATIONAL PARKS AND RESERVES

1. **National Park Tikal:** - One of Guatemala's most famous natural and archeological attractions, Tikal National Park is situated in the center of the Petén Basin and is recognized as a UNESCO World Heritage Site. It includes the historic Mayan city of Tikal, whose lofty pyramids and temples are tucked away in a verdant jungle.

Discover the ancient remains while surrounded by a variety of fauna, such as toucans and howler monkeys.

2. **Biosphere Reserve of Sierra de las Minas:** Numerous habitats, including cloud forests and tropical rainforests, are protected by this enormous biosphere reserve located in eastern Guatemala. It is renowned for having a diverse range of species, including endangered and uncommon ones like the brilliant quetzal. You may get a sense of being completely immersed in nature by hiking around this reserve.

3. The Atitlán Natural Reserve: This reserve, which is near Lake Atitlan, has both cultural value and stunning natural surroundings. Hikers and birdwatchers will find paradise here, as several pathways meander through verdant woodlands. Additionally, the reserve supports sustainable tourism and environmental education.

4. **National Park of Pacaya Volcano:** Hiking this active volcano is exhilarating and is just a short drive from Guatemala City. Hikers may go to the peak to see lava flows and other signs of volcanic activity. Admire the breathtaking sweeping views of neighboring volcanoes from the summit.

5. The Biosphere Reserve of Huehuetenango: Located in Guatemala's western highlands, this reserve is home to a variety of habitats, including cloud forests and highland meadows. For several endangered species, such as the quetzal and the horned guan, it is an essential habitat. Hikers with a bold spirit are drawn to the reserve by its rough terrain.

6. **National Park Volcán Tajumulco:** - Volcán Tajumulco, the tallest summit in Central America, is located in this park. In addition to being a strenuous experience, hiking to the top gives stunning views of the surrounding area, which includes other volcanoes and mountain ranges.

7. **National Park of Rio Dulce:** - Situated on the Caribbean coast by the Rio Dulce River, this park is renowned for its verdant tropical forests, marshes, and varied animals. It's a well-liked location for birding, boating, and river exploration.

8. **Biosphere Reserve Montecristo Trifinio:** - A crucial cloud forest habitat is safeguarded by this transboundary reserve, which is shared by El Salvador and Honduras. Numerous plant and animal species, including ocelots and jaguars, find shelter there. Discover the region's distinctive wildlife and stroll through natural woodlands.

BIRDWATCHING HOTSPOTS

1. Los Tarrales Reserve for birdwatching: Los Tarrales Reserve, which is close to Lake Atitlán, is a birdwatcher's paradise. More than 300 different bird species may be found in the reserve, including the magnificent quetzal, the horned guan, and many toucan species. Paths meander through verdant woods, coffee farms, and the gorgeous lakeside of Atitlán.

2. **National Park Tikal:** - Tikal is a top spot for birding in addition to being well-known for its historic Mayan ruins. Many different species may be found in these jungles, such as parrots, toucans, and trogons. Colorful species like the ocellated turkey and keel-billed toucan are often seen by birdwatchers.

3. **Biosphere Reserve of Sierra de las Minas:** - This sizable reserve in eastern Guatemala is brimming with birds and a hotspot for biodiversity. This area is home to many endangered species, including the horned guan and quetzal. The spot is perfect for birding because of the untouched nature and cloud forests.

4. **Lake Atitlán:** - There are great birding chances around the lake's beaches and in its environs. Many permanent species may be found in the area, and the lake serves as a stopover for migratory birds. Herons, egrets, and kingfishers are among the birds that birdwatchers may encounter.

5. The Huehuetenango Highlands: Guatemala's western highlands are renowned for their untamed scenery and varied wildlife. The blue-throated motmot, azure-rumped tanager, and other highland species may be found in the area. The variety of birds is very great in the Quetzaltenango region.

6. **National Park of Pacaya Volcano:** - Volcano Numerous bird species may be seen living in the woodlands of Pacaya. Hikers who make the trek to the peak may see birds like the beautiful trogon and the volcanic junco. There are plenty of possibilities for birding from the expansive views of the volcano's slopes.

7. **Finca El Pilar:** - This exclusive area close to Antigua is a popular destination for avian enthusiasts. It provides visitors with well-kept pathways that wind through cloud forests, home to unique and migratory species such as collared trogon and emerald toucanet.

8. **Wetlands of Ixcán:** - Wetland habitats in the Ixcán region of northern Guatemala are home to a diverse range of waders and ducks. In this verdant setting, birdwatchers may view kingfishers, jacanas, egrets, and herons.

ACCOMMODATION OPTIONS

LUXURY HOTELS

1. **La Lancha by Coppola** *(Petén)*:

- Located in the heart of the Petén region, near Tikal National Park, La Lancha by Coppola is a luxurious rainforest retreat. This eco-friendly resort offers stylish thatched-roof bungalows overlooking Lake Petén Itzá. Guests can enjoy fine dining at the open-air restaurant, explore nearby Mayan ruins, or relax by the infinity pool surrounded by lush jungle.

2. **Casa Palopó** *(Lake Atitlán)*:

- Situated on the shores of Lake Atitlán in the town of Santa Catarina Palopó, Casa Palopó is a boutique luxury hotel with stunning lake views. The property features beautifully designed rooms, a gourmet restaurant, and a spa. Guests can also visit nearby indigenous villages and take in the breathtaking scenery of the lake and volcanoes.

3. **Las Lagunas Boutique Hotel** *(Flores)*:

- Nestled in the jungle near Flores, Las Lagunas Boutique Hotel is an upscale eco-resort with a unique twist—private overwater bungalows. Each bungalow offers direct access to the Quixel Lagoon, providing a serene and immersive experience in nature. The hotel also features a wildlife rescue center and a restaurant serving international and Guatemalan cuisine.

BOUTIQUE HOTELS

1. **Hotel Casa Santo Domingo** *(Antigua)*:

- Set within the historical city of Antigua, Hotel Casa Santo Domingo is a luxurious boutique hotel housed in a former monastery. It boasts beautiful gardens, art galleries, and several restaurants, making it a charming cultural retreat.

2. **El Convento Boutique Hotel** *(Antigua)*:

- Located in the heart of Antigua, El Convento Boutique Hotel is a beautifully restored 17th-century convent turned into an intimate boutique property. The hotel offers spacious rooms, a tranquil courtyard, and a rooftop terrace with panoramic views of the city and surrounding volcanoes.

3. **Posada del Angel** *(Antigua)*:

- Posada del Angel is a charming boutique hotel in Antigua known for its rustic elegance. The hotel features individually decorated rooms with handmade textiles and artisanal furnishings. The courtyard garden and rooftop terrace provide peaceful spaces for relaxation.

ECO LODGES

1. **Uaxactun Ecolodge** *(Uaxactun)*:

- Uaxactun Ecolodge is an eco-friendly lodge located near the Uaxactun Mayan ruins and Tikal National Park. The lodge offers comfortable accommodations in harmony with the surrounding rainforest. Guests can immerse themselves in nature, explore archaeological sites, and participate in birdwatching tours.

2. **Ixpanpajul Nature Park and Lodge** *(Flores)*:

- Situated within a protected nature park near Flores, Ixpanpajul Lodge offers eco-friendly cabanas nestled in the rainforest canopy. Guests can enjoy canopy walks, zip-lining, and guided tours of the park's diverse flora and fauna.

3. **Earth Lodge** *(Antigua)*:

- Earth Lodge is an eco-lodge located in the hills overlooking Antigua. The property offers unique accommodations in treehouses and adobe-style cabins. Guests can enjoy organic meals, yoga classes, and hiking trails with breathtaking views of the surrounding valleys and volcanoes.

BUDGET HOTELS

1. **Hostal Antigua** *(Antigua)*:

- Hostal Antigua is a budget-friendly hostel in the heart of Antigua. It offers dormitory-style rooms and private accommodations at affordable rates. The hostel has a communal kitchen, and social areas, and is within walking distance of Antigua's attractions.

2. **Los Amigos Hostel** *(Flores)*:

- Located on the island of Flores, Los Amigos Hostel provides budget-friendly accommodation with dormitory and private rooms. The hostel offers a lively atmosphere, a rooftop terrace with lake views, and easy access to the town's restaurants and nightlife.

3. **Ixchel Beach Hotel** *(Panajachel, Lake Atitlán)*:

- Ixchel Beach Hotel is a budget-friendly option on the shores of Lake Atitlán. It offers comfortable rooms with lake views and a restaurant serving local and international cuisine. Guests can relax by the lake or explore the nearby town of Panajachel.

TRANSPORTATION

GETTING THERE

1. Airports: La Aurora International Airport (GUA) in Guatemala City serves as the country's principal international entry point. Major cities in North and Central America send planes to it. Other airports that help with internal and regional travel include Mundo Maya International Airport in Flores, near Tikal, and La Aurora Airport in Guatemala City.

2. *In-country Travel:* Domestic flights are a practical choice for swiftly moving between cities and regions. Airlines that provide links to different locations in Guatemala include Avianca, TAG Airlines, and Maya Island Air. The Tikal ruins are easily accessible by flights to Flores.

By Route:

1. **Highways:** Central America is home to a vast network of roads, including the Pan-American Highway. Road conditions might vary, however, with rural roads often being rougher and major highways usually being well-maintained. Cities like Guatemala City may have heavy traffic.

2. Operating a vehicle: For more autonomous travel, you may rent a vehicle. Be advised that certain locations may have inadequate road signs and that driving at night might be difficult owing to low illumination and unfavorable road conditions. It's wise to use a reliable GPS or map and to be aware of speed restrictions.

3. **Busses:** For intercity travel, public buses and shuttle services are typical. The colorful, repurposed school buses known as "chicken buses" are used for local transportation. For travelers seeking a more comfortable alternative, shuttles are offered on well-traveled routes connecting towns and tourist attractions.

4. **Transportation:** In cities, taxis are commonly accessible and may be booked via applications or by hailing one on the street. Make sure there's a meter on the cab, or haggle over the amount beforehand.

Water:**

1. **Atitlan Lake:** A notable waterway in the highlands is Lake Atitlán and settlements along the lake are often reached by boat. There are both private and public boat cruises available.

2. **Río Dulce:** Offering picturesque boat tours, Río Dulce is located on the Caribbean shore. You may go to the Caribbean Sea, explore the river, and go to Livingston.

3. **Peten Itzá:** Another stunning river is Lake Petén Itzá, which is close to Flores. Boat excursions to Tikal's Mayan ruins are a well-liked option.

GETTING AROUND

There are several methods to navigate Guatemala. The possibilities change based on your anticipated degree of comfort, timeline, and money. Although there aren't many domestic planes, there are plenty of reliable shuttles that can take passengers between well-known locations. There are many rental vehicle options, although in some locations (such as Lake Atitlan), traveling by boat is the most convenient option. In Guatemala, public buses are widely available and provide an affordable, genuine, although congested, mode of transportation.

When You Get There

The first thing you'll need to do when you get to Guatemala is fulfill the admission criteria. For the majority of passengers, this will essentially consist of a passport that is valid for six (6) months beyond the date of arrival and documentation of subsequent or return travel.

Although the weather in this tropical country varies, you may visit it at any time of year. Naturally, the "best time to visit Guatemala" is during its dry season, which runs from November to the beginning of May. The wet season might be more reasonably priced, but it's still really nice. When you plan your journey, bear this in mind.

The quality of domestic airline service in Guatemala is not the finest. Guatemala City and Flores are now the only domestic air routes planned. La Aurora International Airport is the hub for domestic airlines serving Guatemala City (GUA). TACA is the sole airline that flies domestically.

Numerous minor airports around Guatemala are undergoing ongoing upgrades, so it's feasible that in the next few years, domestic flights will provide good access to the nation. In Quetzaltenango, Huehuetenango, Coatepeque, San Marcos, and Puerto San José, new domestic airports are being built. Soon, there could be further airport construction in Retalhuleu and Puerto Barrios.

Using a Rental Car

Renting a vehicle in Guatemala is simple. You may see the nation at your speed with a rental automobile; it's good to have the flexibility and freedom to decide how you want to spend your time. It's a good idea to hire a four-wheel drive automobile if you do decide to rent one, since Guatemalan roads may be unpaved and uneven, particularly in rural regions. Make sure you research your house insurance coverage and determine if you need to get extra insurance. You must have an International Driving Permit (IDP) or a driver's license from your home country to hire a vehicle.

Guatemalan highways sometimes have little signage and may be dangerous. Driving manners are also quite different in Guatemala; for instance, passing on blind bends is not unusual. Use caution while driving a rented automobile throughout this nation.

Via Bus

For most Guatemalans, buses are the primary means of transportation, and many tourists choose to utilize them to save money. These local inter- and intracity buses, also called "chicken buses," are frequently housed in vintage American school buses. You may have to stand the whole bus journey since they can become rather busy. But since they are so cheap, they're a great choice for tourists on a tight budget. They'll also provide you with a genuine experience of the way of life in the Guatemalan community. The buses stop anywhere and go almost anywhere. But keep in mind that there have been mishaps and thefts on public transportation.

Additionally, first-class (primera clase) buses connect Guatemala City, Huehuetenango, Quetzaltenango, Flores, Cobán, and Puerto Barrios, among other important cities. You can count on having a seat on these buses, and some even have toilets. The buses are arranged in roomy, opulent carriages.

By Shuttle

One of the simplest methods to get across Guatemala is via shuttle. These consist of both private and shared transportation, where passengers are dropped off at their hotel at the destination they have chosen and picked up at their hotel at the original location. Typically, shared shuttles provide an hour of waiting time, allowing passengers to pause for lunch or to snap pictures. You may go whenever and anywhere you like with a private shuttle. Service is provided door-to-door by both choices.

By Boat

When visiting Lake Atitlán, Río Dulce, Lake Izabal, or Lívingston, you will probably need to take a boat to get between different locations and points of interest. In these places, there are regular small motorboat services connecting the villages, hotels, and attractions. On Guatemala's Pacific coast, boats are also operated along the Canal de Chiquimulilla.

Via Taxi

You can easily find taxis all across Guatemala. In affluent, touristic districts of bigger cities, taxis may be hailed; in smaller towns, they usually hang around in the center square. Look for a taxi that has a meter. Tuk-tuks, motorized rickshaws, are another kind of transportation available in small communities. These are excellent for short trips and are less expensive than taxis.

You may often work out a daily or weekly tariff with local taxi drivers if you plan to remain in one place longer than the short term and need a method to move about. If you utilize the same driver or firm for many days, you may typically get a reasonable deal. Taxi drivers in Guatemala are kind and courteous.

MAPS AND ITINERARIES

MAPS OF KEY AREAS

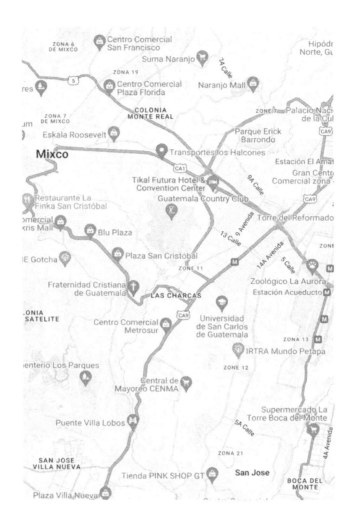

7 DAYS ITINERARIES

Day 1: Guatemala City Arrival

- Touch down in Guatemala City at La Aurora International Airport (GUA).

- After your travel, settle into your accommodation and unwind.

- Discover the city's historic district, pay a visit to Plaza Mayor, and enjoy Guatemalan food at a neighborhood eatery.

Day 2: Guatemala's Antigua

- Make the one-hour trip to Antigua, Guatemala.

- Take in the sights of the Parque Central, the Cathedral, and La Merced Church, all located in the UNESCO-listed historic core.

- Go to the galleries, stores, and marketplaces in your area.

- Savor supper at a restaurant with a rooftop patio and a city view.

Day 3: Volcano Adventure – Set off on an exciting volcanic journey. Opt to climb Acatenango Volcano or Pacaya Volcano.

Take in the breathtaking vistas from the top.

- Come back to Antigua and have a restful evening.

Day 4: Lake Atitlán – Make the 3-hour trip to Lake Atitlán.

- Visit villages around lakes, such as San Pedro la Laguna or Panajachel.

- Take a boat cruise on Lake Atitlan to see the surrounding communities and take in the breathtaking surroundings.

Stay the night at a motel on the lake.

Day 5: Chichicastenango Market

Go to the well-known Chichicastenango Market on Thursdays and Sundays to get a taste of the colorful native culture. See the churches and museums in the town.

- Spend one more night in Lake Atitlan.

Day 6: National Park of Tikal

- Take a 1-hour flight to Flores to explore Tikal National Park.
- Take a look at the imposing pyramids and temples of the Mayan ruins at Tikal.
- Look for animals in the nearby jungle.
Spend the night in Flores.

Day 7: Livingston and Rio Dulce
- Make the 1.5-hour trip to Rio Dulce.
Discover the distinctive Garifuna culture of Livingston and savor the fresh seafood of the region by taking a boat journey down the picturesque Río Dulce canyon and arriving at the town on the Caribbean shore.
- Go back to Rio Dulce for your last evening.

Day 8: Departure – You have the option to continue exploring Rio Dulce or return to Guatemala City by your flight itinerary.

CONCLUSION

As we come to the end on our tour across Guatemala's colorful tapestry, I feel a profound feeling of wonder and kinship with this alluring country. Our journey has been nothing short of amazing, a kaleidoscope of encounters that will always be etched in our memories.

We walked around Antigua's cobblestone streets, feeling the endurance of a country as the echoes of the colonial past reverberated around every turn. We were reminded of the untamed might of nature by the majestic climb of Acatenango and the flaming light of Pacaya's lava flows, which left an indelible impression on our spirits.

While we were immersed in the vivid culture of the indigenous peoples through the brilliant colors and busy bustle of Chichicastenango Market, we were also able to ponder in peace by the reflected waters of Lake Atitlán. The ancient remains of Tikal invited us to reflect on the secrets of the Maya, acting as mute witnesses to millennia past.

I've given you useful advice for seeing this varied country as we've traveled together, from picking the ideal lakefront hotel to relishing Guatemalan food. And for that, I am appreciative of your faith in this guidance.

But this is not where our adventure ends, my traveler. There are many tales to be found, tastes to enjoy, and people to get to know in Guatemala. The country's beauty and intricacy are endless. May the vibrant landscapes of Guatemala encourage you to go further and discover new things—not only in terms of distance but also in terms of your inquisitiveness and awe?

So get back in the bag, listen to your heart, and let the spirit of adventure lead you to new places. Guatemala has shown us that there is a wealth of experiences on the globe just waiting to be fully appreciated.

With unending appreciation for going on this journey with me,

Made in United States
Orlando, FL
03 December 2024

54884881R00059